# Understanding The Mystery Of Destiny

## MOSES OMOJOLA

ISBN-13:978-1522802754
ISBN-10:1522802754

# DEDICATION

To every determined person who wants to step out of
confusion and get the right answers to the following life
baffling questions: *Who am I?* Why am I here? *Where do I
suppose to be? What work do I suppose to be doing? What career
do I suppose to pursue? What problem am I created to solve? Who
am I sent to? What is my Destiny? What is my life Purpose?
What is my Calling? What is my Divine Assignment? What is
my Vision and Life Mission? How can I fulfill my Destiny?*

# CONTENTS

# ACKNOWLEDGMENTS

I am grateful to the hundreds of writers and teachers both classical and contemporary, who have shaped my life and helped me learn these truths.

Unlimited thanks goes to my beloved wife, Deborah Ojute, for her love, encouragement and timely advice that led to the publishing of this book.

My greatest appreciation goes to my Creator, His only Son, and the Holy Spirit for revealing to me how I have been wired to affect my generation.

# 1 DESTINY FOUNDATION

You and I must ever be grateful to God for creating us to dwell on the earth that He framed into being through His Word.

God's Word says:

**Ps 24:1**

*The earth is the LORD's, and the fulness thereof; the world, and they that dwell therein.*

*God created man after he spoke into being all the things that will make life comfortable for him.*

Let's examine God's utterance that made man to evolve on earth.

**Gen 1:26**

*Let us make man in our image, in our likeness, and let them rule over the fish of the sea and the birds of the air, over the livestock, over all the earth, and over all the creatures that move along the ground.*

So, God proceeded and created man in his own image, gave him dominion and blessed him.

God blessed them and said to them:

## Gen 1:28

*Be fruitful and increase in number; fill the earth and subdue it. Rule over the fish of the sea and the birds of the air and over every living creature that moves on the ground.*

When God formed man He provided everything that man needed to survive.

## Gen 2:8-9

*Now the LORD God had planted a garden in the east, in Eden; and there he put the man he had formed. And the LORD God made all kinds of trees grow out of the ground trees that were pleasing to the eye and good for food.*

The evidence of God's providence for man is also confirmed in the scripture below:

## Gen 2:10-12

*Now a river went out of Eden to water the garden, and from there it parted and became four riverheads. The name of the first is Pishon; it is the one which skirts the whole land of Havilah, where there is gold. And the gold of that land is good. Bdellium and the onyx stone are there.*

"The gold of that land is good" So God planned that we should enjoy the fullness of His glory, lacking nothing. God's plan was for us to work with ease. It is not His plan that human being should live on jobs. He created each of us for a specific task, which he intended each person to do with ease and little labour.

## Gen 2:15

*And the LORD God took the man, and put him into the Garden of Eden to dress it and to keep it.*

This scripture tells us that God placed Adam and Eve in the Garden of Eden for the purpose of simply dressing and keeping the garden. This implies that there is a task God wants each person to carry out or handle on earth. God predetermined a need in your generation and He has designed you accurately to meet that need.

Frankly speaking, only you can handle the assignment God has created you to fulfill, as your own part of His universal destiny.

Despite this perfect plan of God that we should enjoy our stay on earth, the first sin crept in. This sin was passed on to you and I, and needed redress. Hear it yourself:

## Rom 3:23

*For all have sinned and fall short of the glory of God*

When Serpent made Adam and Eve to fall short of the glory of God, God drove them out of the Garden of Eden, and change their living status.

## Gen 2:7

*And the LORD God formed man of the dust of the ground, and breathed into his nostrils the breath of life; and man became a living being.*

## Gen 3:23

*Therefore the LORD God sent him out of the Garden of Eden to till the ground from which he was taken.*

Two things happened to Adam and Eve at this stage of their lives. Firstly, they were removed from the environment that they understood, which was specially designed for them to receive God's will on earth as it is in heaven – The life of comfort, success and fruitfulness.

Secondly, God reduced them to a living synonymous to carnivorous, that is, a life of tilling the ground from which they were taken.

Man tilling the ground from which he was taken is equivalent to, you and I, destroying or inflicting injury on our own bodies before we eat daily. I am convinced; you know the great pain you will feel if you cut your skin with razor repeatedly!

I see living on jobs as consequence of Adam's sin and the resultant effect of being thrown out of God's radar.

Now compare the work God planned for man originally: "Dressing a garden and keeping it" to "Tilling the ground from where he was taken"

In your Secondary School days, or elsewhere, you must have seen a Gardener. You discover that Gardeners never do any tedious job. They work with ease. You hardly see a gardener work under the sun. He may not even sweat while working, because he does not work under duress. He chooses when to do his work. The whole of his work is trimming of flowers or cutting of grasses, selectively, at his chosen time and discretion.

You dare not compare his kind of work to that of a farmer or a tree feller in the bush or a wheelbarrow pusher in a third world country home market.

What am I saying? I mean Gods intention was not for

us to suffer or labour hard before we get our daily bread. God created food to depend on us, not we depend on food.

What about that age-long mystery? It may please you to know that a mystery occurred when Adam and Eve left Eden, which continued to trouble man till today.

When Adam and Eve were relieved of their original work of dressing the garden and keeping it – their divine assignment and mission on earth, they were taking off balance. Consequently, their names were no longer found in the employment list of God and the devil decided to enlist them in the world labour market. In this state, they had to depend on their head, faulty thoughts, and satanic leading for survival. And the best Satan could offer them was job instead of work. This is how the whole world came about the term job instead of work.

Have you ever found the word job in the Holy Bible? The word 'job' with respect to means of living is an orchestration of the devil.

I define **Job** as what the world system provide for you as a means of living.

**WORK** is your divine assignment or mission on earth channeled towards your path of destiny. Your work is what God gives you to catapult you into satisfaction, fulfillment, wealth, and inner peace. In summary, it places you on a life of significance.

When you discover and do what God made you to do

on earth, you are said to be 'working', and heaven will begin to testify daily about you, as it testified about Jesus at his baptism in Jordan, and at the mount of transfiguration.

## Matt 3:17

*And suddenly a voice came from heaven, saying, "This is My beloved Son, in whom I am well pleased."*

## Matt 17:5

*While he was still speaking, behold, a bright cloud overshadowed them; and suddenly a voice came out of the cloud, saying, "This is My beloved Son, in whom I am well pleased. Hear Him!"*

When you do the work God made you for, God will not only be pleased with you, He will make you an authority in that field. People will gather around you because their needs are met. They will marvel at your wisdom and your gifting. You will have extra strength and peace in your spirit.

But when you live on jobs, it will result in you living from hand to mouth, lack of steady employment, lack of inner peace, and instability in your matrimonial capital base.

Hello! You may be wealthy but not really successful. This is because you are in the wrong place of your divine assignment. What does that mean? If you have money, wealth, possession or prestige outside the work God predestined you to do on earth, you will lack fulfillment, satisfaction, significance and inner peace.

Simply put:

Success is doing what God made you to do! It is evident by inner peace and passion.

**Prov 10:22**

*The blessing of the LORD makes one rich, and He adds no sorrow with it.*

# Destiny In Christ

As a result of unlimited and ever increasing compassion of God, and His tender mercies, which are over all His works, He sent His only begotten son to redeem us to Him.

**Rom 3:23-24**

*Being justified freely by His grace through the redemption that is in Christ Jesus*

**Eph 1:7**

*In Him we have redemption through His blood, the forgiveness of sins, according to the riches of His grace.*

Through the blood of Jesus, you have the grace to recover whatever you have lost as a result of the sudden evacuation of Adam and Eve from the Garden of Eden.

## Eph 1:11

*In Him also we have obtained an inheritance, being predestined according to the purpose of Him who works all things according to the counsel of His will.*

Jesus is the only way. Through His light, you can navigate yourself into your designed purpose in life. Now let us consider these two scriptures:

## John 3:16

*For God so loved the world that He gave His only begotten Son, that whoever believes in Him should not perish but have everlasting life.*

## 1 John 3:16

*By this we know love, because He laid down His life for us. And we also ought to lay down our lives for the brethren.*

God loved us. You and I were off His radar for a long time. In His infinite mercy He sent His son with great risk to die for our sins so as to bring us back to Him. He expects us to show appreciation too by laying down our lives. For who? - Those whom He has destined us to serve through our niche in our life journey, also through our giving attitude, in the worship of God. Giving is serving, and serving is giving. This is termed servant leadership.

This is explained further below.

Paul, an apostle of Jesus Christ writing to the Holy and faithful brothers in Christ at Colosse said:

## Col 4:17(KJV)

*And say to Archippus, Take heed to the ministry which thou hast received in the Lord, that thou fulfil it.*

## Col 4:17 (NIV)

*Tell Archippus: "See to it that you complete the work you have received in the Lord."*

There is a pre-determined work or assignment God has given to you and spoken into your life to fulfill while on earth. He has also mandated you to accomplish this task with all vigour. You have your own part of the entire destiny in Christ Jesus to fulfill during your short time of sojourn on earth.

Jesus was very conscious of his destiny, His purpose, divine assignment and mission while on earth. He was so committed to fulfilling His purpose that He refused to allow anyone, no matter how close to Him, to stand between Him and His destiny. Remember, He rebuked Peter who was His closest associate:

In the book of Mark 8:33, Jesus rebuked Peter, saying, "Get behind Me, Satan! For you are not mindful of the things of God, but the things of men."

Jesus came to die for mankind and redeem man to his Creator. Jesus' commitment to His work is buttressed by His submission to working even on Sabbath day. The world calls this overtime. But Jesus was not even on salary. Little wonder, Apostle Paul said he worked night and day.

I am not saying that you should use the time for church service for other things on Sunday. I am only telling you how committed Jesus was in fulfilling His destiny on earth. Of course, Jesus made us to understand that there is nothing wrong in using Sunday in other way, as long as it is to the glory of God – Healing on the Sabbath day glorifies God. So He used it in that way. Now, hear master Jesus:

## John 4:34

*"My food," said Jesus, "is to do the will of him who sent me and to finish his work.*

## John 9:4-5

*I must work the works of Him who sent Me while it is day; the night is coming when no one can work. As long as I am in the world, I am the light of the world."*

Your food should be in your divine assignment, not on that nasty thing called job.

# 2 LOCATE WHERE YOU BELONG AND GIVE IT ALL YOU'VE GOT

So, what next? You locate where you belong: your niche, your best fit in life, and give it all you've got, that's all. Jesus has given you the light to work with and you must make haste while the sun shine.

Again, Jesus was so committed to fulfilling His divine assignment that he broke protocol. He knew God would blame Him if He refused to heal those who needed healing on Sabbath days. So He chose to please God rather than please men or better still, the Sadducees, Pharisees and the Scribes. He broke the Jewish tradition. He showed believers plainly that the Sabbath day can be used in a spiritually led way, to the glory of God provided it is not for personal gain.

I read a book, in which the author said that when the prophets of old are at the point of delivering God's message, the Spirit torment them in such a way that they manifest momentary madness. I mean, the Spirit exact a strange force on them, that, their behaviour and character would fit perfectly into that of a mad man.

Wake up! Your passion must surpass that of Christ whom you are modelling. Be obsessive to your passion.

Furthermore, the proposition that you will make heaven depends largely on your fruitfulness towards God on earth. God, in His own heart, has tied your accruing fruitfulness to your Work or assignment on earth, not your job, career, profession, which are usually, selfishly stomach driven. This is the life of serving and giving which He has equipped you adequately for:

## Heb 12:2

*Looking unto Jesus, the author and finisher of our faith, who for the joy that was set before Him endured the cross, despising the shame, and has sat down at the right hand of the throne of God.*

God – the Father, the Son, and the Holy Sprit is ready to pilot you to fulfill your assignment on earth so that later, in the life to come, you will say: Heaven here I come.

# What Did Christ Say Unto You?

Jesus told his disciples that the Holy Ghost would teach them all things and bring all things to their remembrance, whatsoever He has said unto them.

## John 14:26

But the Comforter, which is the Holy Ghost, whom the Father will send in my name, he shall teach you all things, and bring all things to your remembrance, whatsoever I have said unto you.

In this context, what Jesus was referring to was what He has spoken into their life before they were created into this obnoxious world. Here, I am talking about speaking forth and foundations. Which foundations? Foundation of the world and your own foundation too, I mean your world as an individual.

Here again, I am referring to you being foreknown and your future being predetermined. The Bible says Christ is the Word and the Word existed even before man was created.

To be candid, John reported that all things were made by Him. So Christ knows all the details about your destiny.

## John 1:1-4

*In the beginning was the Word, and the Word was with God, and the Word was God. The same was in the beginning with God. All things were made by him; and without him was not any thing made that was made. In him was life; and the life was the light of men.*

Paul said in the book of Ephesians that God has chosen us in him before the foundation of the world.

## Eph 1:4

*According as he hath chosen us in him before the foundation of the world, that we should be holy and without blame before him in love:*

If you believe that Jesus Christ was foreordained before the foundation of the world, then, you too was planned and designed for a purpose and unique assignment.

Your destiny cap can only fit you perfectly and no one else in the world running into billions of people. You are a perfect engine more glorious that aggregate of terrestrial machines put together.

Jesus existed at the time of creation of the universe; He only came into the world to manifest in the flesh form for the purpose of redemption.

## 1 Peter 1:20

*Who verily was foreordained before the foundation of the world, but was manifest in these last times for you.*

## John 1:14

*And the Word was made flesh, and dwelt among us, (and we beheld his glory, the glory as of the only begotten of the Father,) full of grace and truth.*

## John 17:24

*Father, I will that they also, whom thou hast given me, be with me where I am; that they may behold my glory, which thou hast given me: for thou lovedst me before the foundation of the world.*

# A Vision On How You Came Into This World

Before your Creator introduced you into this world and the generation that you are part of now, an event took place that you were not conscious of. It occurred in your nonexistence.

Beloved, if you will agree with me, the spirit that gave birth to your being was without nomenclature. This means that, the spirit had no bearing to you at that point in question. Simply put, that spirit was undefined.

Now, there is what I call 'Divine Summoning'. Through divine summoning, God summoned a spirit to the midst of those with him, with the purpose of handling a task in a specific generation on earth. They needed to speak this divine task into the summoned

24

spirit. Now just like what happened in revelation chapter five, as revealed to John, none of those fellowshipping with God at that point in time was capable of speaking to, or sending forth that spirit on the assignment except our Lord Jesus Christ.

## Rev 5:1-7

*And I saw in the right hand of Him who sat on the throne a scroll written inside and on the back, sealed with seven seals. Then I saw a strong angel proclaiming with a loud voice, "Who is worthy to open the scroll and to loose its seals?" And no one in heaven or on the earth or under the earth was able to open the scroll, or to look at it. So I wept much, because no one was found worthy to open and read the scroll, or to look at it. But one of the elders said to me, "Do not weep. Behold, the Lion of the tribe of Judah, the Root of David, has prevailed to open the scroll and to loose its seven seals." And I looked, and behold, in the midst of the throne and of the four living creatures, and in the midst of the elders, stood a Lamb as though it had been slain, having seven horns and seven eyes, which are the seven Spirits of God sent out into all the earth. Then He came and took the scroll out of the right hand of Him who sat on the throne.*

Here, in the book of Revelation, It was said that there was no competent person to open the scroll that was sealed with seven seals, until a Lamb that seems slain appeared and volunteered, took the scroll, and began to open the seals one after the other.

In like manner, our Lord Jesus Christ volunteered and spoke 'you' into the spirit that became you. The you in quote are your destiny and assignment. Jesus told that spirit the unique task he would be coming to the world to do. Jesus enumerated all that the spirit must accomplish on earth before returning home.

Do you know what Jesus said to the spirit? Jesus must have said:

We are sending you to generation X in planet earth, to solve problem Y. We have shaped you, modeled your make –up and equipped you to handle this problem effectively and tactically with ease. Furthermore, these are the details you need to accomplish the simplified task... You must make sure you complete the task in the set time we would allow you to stay there. Failure to complete the assignment means that you will no longer be part of us. We have designed your DNA and packaged you appropriately to fulfill this divine assignment. Whether you succeed or you fail, it will be your fault. Receive grace. Receive something for nothing. Receive unmerited favour. Receive God riches at Christ expense. Now, I charge you, Go! Go!! Go!!! to the world and affect your generation.

So after Jesus Christ has spoken to the spirit, which before then was just a certain spirit, its divine assignment and destiny, God then commanded the spirit to enter into a mass of clay molded in human form. Then this assigned spirit began to cohabit with a body and a soul, which became human being. By God's sovereignty, God now chose a womb for the development of the organism planned to be introduced into the world, as a little child, after a period of nine months. That's your foundation.

## Forgotten Assignment

Did it ever happen to you as a little child probably in the ghetto, that your father, mother or guardian sent you to deliver a message to somebody, but before you reach the recipient, you could no longer remember the message? This is the scenario with all men concerning their destiny.

Because of the absence of the soul - the cerebrum, cerebellum and medulla oblongata, when Jesus rolled out the unique assignment to the Spirit, the resulting human being had no knowledge or consciousness of what happened to his Spirit ahead of time. So you see why your body, soul and spirit have no knowledge of your divine destiny or life purpose.

Therefore everything pertaining to your destiny, mission and life purpose became a mystery or unknown. Hence Jesus often makes reference to the need for believers to understand mystery, when he was on earth.

Destiny is different from purpose. Destiny is restricted to human usage and is end pertinent, purpose is not. So I prefer the word destiny rather than purpose, for purpose may not have future ambition and accomplishment.

## Mark 4:11-12

*And he said unto them, Unto you it is given to know the mystery of the kingdom of God: but unto them that are without, all these things are done in parables: That seeing they may see, and not perceive; and hearing they may hear, and not understand; lest at any time they should be converted, and their sins should be forgiven them.*

# Transfer Of Baton

The only person that bears record of your destiny on earth is Jesus Christ, but He ascended to heaven over two thousand years ago. However, darling Jesus said you should not bother about His absence in this world; He therefore assigned a colleague of His - the Comforter, called the Holy Spirit, to reveal to you every detail concerning your destiny.

## John 14:26

*But the Comforter, which is the Holy Ghost, whom the Father will send in my name, he shall teach you all things, and bring all things to your remembrance, whatsoever I have said unto you.*

Jesus Christ sees you, as king and priest, and he want you to reign as leader in your best -fit- in -life.

## Rev 5:10

*And hast made us unto our God kings and priests: and we shall reign on the earth.*

Christ has given you all spiritual blessings, but He attached their manifestation to your divine assignment. Below are the seven key things you stand to receive when you discover your destiny and walk on the path of fulfilling that purpose:

## Rev 5:12

*Saying with a loud voice, worthy is the Lamb that was slain to receive power, and riches, and wisdom, and strength, and honour, and glory, and blessing.*

# 3 CLIMBING YOUR LADDER TO REAL SUCCESS

## The Meaning of Destiny

Destiny is the living out of God's purposes, within your life span. As a man of destiny, God designed you to fulfill your divine destiny through your Calling. Your calling will manifest in the form of the work you do, your occupation, business, vocation, profession, passion, mission or divine assignment.

Many erroneously define destiny as a lofty spiritual goal, which only a few are chosen to fulfill, the way you go about your daily life and the style of living you engage in, the direction in which your growth is unfolding either toward fulfillment and love or toward confusion and despair.

From scripture: Jer 1:5-12, we observe that your being a blessing to your generation can only be fulfilled through service to humanity which you must be busy doing by serving in the area of your assignment. Therefore, your assignment is your life mission or your predetermined work or tasks in life. It is indicated by your passions and unexplainable happenings, divine diversion and divine interventions in your life. Simply put, it is an assignment God has consecrated, ordained, predestined and designed you to accomplish.

It is the only avenue God authorizes you to serve your generation. God will not reward you when you operate outside your designed domain, that is, destiny domain. You don't need any special qualification or better still, paper qualification to occupy your pre - designed place of destiny. All that God require first from you are your availability and commitment. Developing yourself along your path of destiny can follow suit. I'm going to ask you now: Are you available for your assignment or you still want to remain in the status quo?

I knew one man of God in some time past. He only attended primary school, which I wasn't convinced he completed. I had the opportunity of listening to this man of God several times when he preached to his congregation. He preached eloquently, using vocabulary freely at will. We who were academic scholars could not puncture his speech for grammatical error.

I came to grip one day and feared God the more, when this great preacher could not write a 'simple' letter to his family member, and had to call a graduate in that ministry to help him write the informal letter.

Wake up! Stop discouraging yourself. Who said you are not qualified? You are the most qualified person for the task God sent you to fulfill in your generation. Only you can stop yourself, even the enemies of your father's house cannot stop you, because they weren't there when Jesus spoke to the spirit that birth your DNA.

The first journey God want you to go on earth is the journey of discovering who you are and your assignment. This bold step can then be backed up with casting your life vision, equipping, Mentoring, and funding. God on His own will supply you with power, authority and strength that you need to fulfill your destiny. Your creator is eager and willing to support you to enable you complete your destiny in the set time He has chosen for you – your life span.

## What You Must Know

Let's ponder on this scripture:

And we know that all things work together for good to

them that love God, to them who are the called according to his purpose.

For whom he did foreknow, he also did predestinate to be conformed to the image of his Son, that he might be the firstborn among many brethren.

## Rom 8:28-30

*Moreover whom he did predestinate, them he also called: and whom he called, them he also justified: and whom he justified, them he also glorified.*

For all things to work together for good in your life and for you to be really successful in life, there are two things you must do:

1. You must love God.

2. You must be at your place of assignment.

Verse 28 of this scripture also reveal that everything that has happened to you from birth is orchestrated by God to enable you fulfill your destiny.

To every man on earth, there is a foreknown and predestination. Concerning you in particular, there was a Foreknown before you were predestinated. There was a foreseen and a foreknown about you. The foreseen is the problem God saw in your generation and has created you beforehand and equipped you to solve. The foreknow means that God knew your make –up, He knows who He made you to be. He knows your ability. He indicated this in his communication with great men like Gideon, Jeremiah and Moses. To foreknow is to ordain or know beforehand. In clarity, the foreseen and the foreknow refer to the problem and the man destined to solve the problem respectively.

To Gideon, hear what God said:

## Judg 6:12

*And the angel of the LORD appeared unto him, and said unto him, The LORD is with thee, thou mighty man of valour.*

To Jeremiah the Lord said:

## Jer 1:5

*Before I formed thee in the belly I knew thee; and before thou camest forth out of the womb I sanctified thee, and I ordained thee a prophet unto the nations.*

And to Moses, when he complained of stammering:

## Ex 4:10-12

*And Moses said unto the LORD, O my Lord, I am not eloquent, neither heretofore, nor since thou hast spoken unto thy servant: but I am slow of speech, and of a slow tongue. And the LORD said unto him, Who hath made man's mouth? or who maketh the dumb, or deaf, or the seeing, or the blind? have not I the LORD? Now therefore go, and I will be with thy mouth, and teach thee what thou shalt say.*

My beloveth, the most valuable son God has is Jesus Christ and God's plan is that you should be like him. Jesus Christ lived a life of significance, fulfillment, and fruitfulness throughout His stay on earth.

In John's account of Jesus' miraculous feeding of five thousand men, John recorded that He was not confused about what to do, when they had only five barley loaves and two fishes to feed that ridiculous number. Phillip, Andrew and the rest of the disciples were confused and worried, but He was not. John said, "For he know what He would do". Worry or anxiety is not of God.

## John 6:5-6

*When Jesus then lifted up his eyes, and saw a great company come unto him, he saith unto Philip, Whence shall we buy bread that these may eat? And this he said to prove him: for he himself knew what he would do.*

God's desire is that you live a life of bliss - Life without lack; having power, possessions and money to the glory of God. The choice is then yours whether to live a life of rigorous discipleship like the one lived by Jesus Christ or a life of responsible consumption. Which one do you prefer? Or do you want to live a life of consuming all that you ever produced. I advice you, don't live such life because, people who live only for what to consume end up being consumed in the process.

I'm also pleased to announce to you that the scripture we are considering in the book of Romans makes us to understand that God designed you to be great leader in your generation. When you locate your best-fit-in-life, your niche or divine place of assignment, you become a much sought after person like Jesus. Jesus started his meaningful life in the wilderness, in solitude. Later He led twelve. He graduated into leading seventy and then multitudes. So it is with men of destiny.

## Rom 8:29

*For whom he did foreknow, he also did predestinate to be conformed to the image of his Son, that he might be the firstborn among many brethren.*

## The Four Ladders To Real Success

Now on your way to real success in life, there are four ladders you must climb, acknowledging God's Power, Might and Spirit. These ladders are: Ladder of Predestination, Calling, Justification, and Glorification. At the completion of the third ladder; justification, you will just be prospering anyhow.

From today, I see you prospering unhindered in Jesus' name.

## Predestination

The word predestination is translated "predestined" in scripture referenced below, and it is from the Greek word 'proorizo', which carries the meaning of "to determine beforehand," "to ordain", "to decide upon ahead of time." So, predestination is God determining certain things to occur ahead of time. Now, what did God determine ahead of time?

## Rom 8:29

*For whom He foreknew, He also predestined to be conformed to the image of His Son, that He might be the firstborn among many brethren.*

God predetermined that certain individuals would be conformed to the likeness of His Son, be called, justified, and glorified. In particular, predestination concerns God's decision to create and to govern Creation, and the extent to which God's decision determines ahead of time what the destiny of groups and individuals will be. Before God creates, He decides to do it.

Paul refers to Jacob and Esau. Before they were even born, before they had done any good or evil, God decreed in advance that the elder would serve the younger: "Jacob have I loved; Esau have I hated." The point there is that God had chosen certain benefits for one of those two before they were even born.

The real debate is, on what basis does God predestinate? We know that he predestines, but why does he predestine, and what is the basis for his choices? God knows in advance what people are going to do, what choices they are going to make, what activities they're going to be involved in. As he looks through the corridor of time and knows what choices you will make, for example, he knows that you will hear the gospel. He knows whether you will say no or yes, then he chose you for salvation on the basis of this prior knowledge.

## Rom 9:12-13

*"The older will serve the younger." Just as it is written: "Jacob I loved, but Esau I hated."*

Now, let us look at two scriptures below:

## Eph 1:5

*Having predestined us to adoption as sons by Jesus Christ to Himself, according to the good pleasure of His will,*

## Eph 1:11

*In Him also we have obtained an inheritance, being predestined according to the purpose of Him who works all things according to the counsel of His will…,*

To every man God created there is a foreknown or predestination. He told prophet Jeremiah:

## Jer 1:5

*"Before I formed you in the womb I knew you;*

*Before you were born I sanctified you;*

*I ordained you a prophet to the nations."*

God also told Gideon that He knew the ability he has put in his DNA.

## Judg 6:12

*And the Angel of the LORD appeared to him, and said to him, "The LORD is with you, you mighty man of valor!"*

Gideon showed inferiority complex when God was sending him to the war front because he was ignorant of himself. So many people are like that today. They are bothered by the grasshopper image of the book of Numbers chapter 13. Relying on evil report of incompetence.

## Num 13:27-28

*Here is its fruit. But the people who live there are powerful, and the cities are fortified and very large.*

If the inhabitant of Canaan were really powerful, how were they able to come to Moses with fruit of the land? Seed of discouragement. Little wonder God told Gideon, go in this mirth. I believe, God told David the same thing, though David did not tell Saul, when Saul wore David a complete war apron.

## Judg 6:14-15

*Then the LORD turned to him and said, "Go in this might of yours, and you shall save Israel from the hand of the Midianites. Have I not sent you?" So he said to Him, "O my Lord, how can I save Israel? Indeed my clan is the weakest in Manasseh, and I am the least in my father's house."*

I am sure Gideon didn't believe God until God asked him to turn back thirty one thousand seven hundred people and defeated the Midianites with just 300. Small but mighty. In the war against the Midianites, out of thirty two thousand Israelites selected to go to the war fronts, God instructed that twenty two thousand that were fearful should go back home from the battlefront. Of the ten thousand men remaining God still instructed that nine thousand seven hundred should go back after an unusual test on drinking of water.

Beloveth, you need a big heart and total dependence on God in order to work with him in focus and complete what He has called you to do.

## Judg 7:7

*Then the LORD said to Gideon, "By the three hundred men who lapped I will save you, and deliver the Midianites into your hand.*

Now, let's consider this scripture:

## Jer 18:3-6

*Then I went down to the potter's house, and there he was, making something at the wheel. And the vessel that he made of clay was marred in the hand of the potter; so he made it again into another vessel, as it seemed good to the potter to make... then the word of the LORD came to me, saying: "O house of Israel, can I not do with you as this potter?" says the LORD. "Look, as the clay is in the potter's hand, so are you in My hand, O house of Israel!*

The scripture above teaches that you must be broken, and fully in tune with the Holy Spirit. God shaped human beings to various make-ups according to the plan and purpose He wants them to accomplish on earth.

God revealed to Joseph how great he has predestined him to be at the age of 17 even when he has not attained the skills of managing dreams, in a household full of envy. God wants to teach us at all time, So He welcomes those who are broken enough to be taught and delights in them.

## Gen 37:9

*Then he dreamed still another dream and told it to his brothers, and said, "Look, I have dreamed another dream. And this time, the sun, the moon, and the eleven stars bowed down to me."*

Before our Lord and saviour, Jesus Christ was born, God revealed his coming to the world through prophet Isaiah, and he made a complete description of him:

## Isa 9:6-7

*For unto us a Child is born,*

*Unto us a Son is given; and the government will be upon His shoulder.*

*And His name will be called*

*Wonderful, Counselor, Mighty God,*

*Everlasting Father, Prince of Peace.*

*Of the increase of His government and peace*

*There will be no end, upon the throne of David and over His kingdom,*

*To order it and establish it with judgment and justice.*

It is relevant to say here too, that before you were born into this world, some privileged people or prophets knew beforehand of your coming. I am not talking of people like king Herod.

The book of Genesis reveals that after God created everything that would sustain life on earth, there was a let us before He took the decision to create man and brought him into existence. Meaning man did not evolve on his own as some evolution theories postulated.

## Gen 1:26-27

*Then God said, "Let Us make man in Our image, according to Our likeness; let them have dominion over the fish of the sea, over the birds of the air, and over the cattle, over all the earth and over every creeping thing that creeps on the earth." So God created man in His own image; in the image of God He created him; male and female He created them.*

God is a sovereign God. He does things the way He wants.

## Eph 1:11-12

*In Him also we have obtained an inheritance, being predestined according to the purpose of Him who works all things according to the counsel of His will*

Now that you know that there was a predestination concerning your life, you need to ask yourself: What did God speak in advance concerning my life before I was born? Ask yourself again: What am I here for? May be you also want to ask yourself: Apart from

Jesus Christ and the Holy Spirit, who else around me were present at my creation, who knows about my destiny, my make-up, or my purpose of existence?

What will I use to illustrate destiny again? Holy Spirit help me! Your destiny refers to your end- point or the summation of your living on earth and how you are able to affect your generation.

I remember those days, as student of chemistry in secondary school and in the university. In chemistry, an acid will react with a base to produce salt and water. In titration experiment, a certain quantity of acid stored in a burette is carefully and gradually introduced in bits into a known base, which has been poured earlier into a conical flask by means of a pipette. The student Chemist stops adding the acid to the base as soon as the mixture turns purple. Scientist calls this End - point. When this end-point is accurately determined, the student is elated so also the teacher will gladly award mark to the student.

In like manner, you must live your life mastering the artistry of combining mandatory precautions with your divine assignment in order to get at your end-point. This end-point is the inter-phase that makes you cross over as eligible candidate of heaven. I see you overcoming and attaining that fit in Jesus' name.

I must state here again, that you must love God. Loving God whom you do not see, and His dear son, Jesus Christ implies that you show that love to someone else, 'the little ones' around you. Now, who are the little ones? I defined them in this context to be the biblical 'neighbours'. The little ones are those in need, be it physical, spiritual or emotional needs. They need care. Jesus sees them as being helpless and orphans. They don't have to be members of your congregation or Christians before you extend that love of Christ to them. Maybe the help you give in an instance, without grudge, is all that that unbeliever needs, as bait, to lead him to Christ. Sometimes when I say this, some wonderful men of God reject this Holy Spirit led teaching of mine! By religion the Good Samaritan was not as righteous as the

Levite and the Priest. But I am persuaded that Jesus will give His verdict in my favour concerning this statement. God is no respecter of persons.

You must serve humanity in your designed area. God knew you before you were born and He has modeled you in line with Jesus Christ. God wants you to be leader in the work he has predetermined you to do, that is why you are the first born among many brethren, I repeat. Ask yourself, what do I give back to God through serving my generation? My beloved, can you remember the food you ate two weeks ago? No way. Hello, if you have given that same food to somebody in need, not only will he remember the food, he will also remember that person who did Christ for him. I charge you, learn to do Christ for people. For that person that gave food to the man in need, Yoruba beggars says he gave such alms to Christ, not they who beg for the alms! They are quoting scripture, Matthew chapter twenty-five.

## Matt 25:40

*And the King will answer and say to them, 'Assuredly, I say to you, inasmuch as you did it to one of the least of these My brethren, you did it to Me.*

"E ta Jesu lore" Means 'give alms to Jesus. This is the message Yoruba beggars pass across to listeners as they go about begging for alms. May be you need to go to the western part of Nigeria to confirm this. What a great faith shown by those you may think you are more righteous than.

# BOOK TAGS

meaning of life, goal setting, purpose of life, on purpose, purpose, self improvement, self confidence, career change, career counseling, dream meaning, my destiny, my future, destiny, leadership skills, looking for a job, careers, career counseling, healing scriptures, scriptures on healing, goal setting, purpose of life, self improvement, destiny, leadership skills, looking for a job, careers, divine intervention, sermons, health and wellness, getting pregnant, vision, the vision, what does my dream mean, depression treatment, my destiny, dream meaning, purpose of life, careers, dreams, vision, how to choose a career, choosing career, vision statement, my destiny, job search, dream meaning, what is the purpose of life, on purpose, purpose of life, destiny, vision statement, career change, career counseling, career coaching, healing prayer, prayers for strength, how to choose a career, choosing career, career finder, vision statement, my destiny, job search, dream meaning, what is the purpose of life, mission and vision, what does my dream mean, leadership training, how to choose a career, choosing career, career finder, vision statement, my destiny, job search, dream meaning, what is the purpose of life, mission and vision, what does my dream mean, career coach, ordained, christian counseling, human rights, leadership training, social justice issues, divine intervention, church of christ, spiritual gifts test, ordained, evangelist, youth group, family christian store, morning devotions, christian counseling, career coach, power of prayer, bible study, bible studies, find a job, job opportunities, job seekers, leadership development, sermons, sermon, success stories, success story, the holy spirit, business opportunity, business opportunities, rehab, social anxiety, retirement planning, pastor, christian dating, evening prayer, morning prayer, health and wellness, health and fitness, christian, dream interpretation, dream interpretation, symptoms of depression, symptoms of anxiety, signs of depression, what is the purpose of life, what is the meaning of life, symptoms of stress, stress symptoms, how to relieve stress, how to reduce stress, how to manage stress, how to cope with stress

# For Comments, Coaching and Consulting Jobs:

## To help you:

- Discover your destiny or life purpose, Cast life Vision and Goals.
- Discover 3-4 profitable businesses you are created to do to have wealth, live healthy and have inner peace.
- Teach you how to write book, write great, voluminous and over 20 books.
- Self-publish your book for you.
- Convert your book to Ebook and Audiobook, upload and sell on Amazon, Barnes & Noble, Apple store, Kobo, Audible.com, Clickbank, ACX, etc.
- Promote your books & services for you on Internet.
- Give you counsel on life issues, business and health matters, book writing, publishing, sales and marketing.
- Create simple Website and Blog for you.

# List of Moses Omojola books available in paperback, ebook, audiobook format on Amazon US & UK:

1. How To Break Into Your Calling

2. Understanding The Mystery of Destiny

3. How to activate the miracles in your spirit

4. How to navigate into success and significance

5. Flight To Destiny: The roadmap to your destiny

6. Repositioning The Church: Morals And Teachings

7. How To Pray In The Holy Ghost And Win All Battles

8. How To Solve Your Problems Through Your Destiny

9. Destiny Pilot 1: Unplanned Pregnancy; What Not To Do

10. Destiny Pilot 2: Unplanned Pregnancy: What To Do (1)

11. Destiny Pilot 3: Unplanned Pregnancy: What To Do (2)

12. How To Harmonize Your Destiny With Divine Intervention

13. How To Cope With Thorns In The Flesh: Exploit

Of Grace

14. Prayer To Discover Your Purpose and Start Your Ministry

15. Leadership and Sin Intervention: How Not To Treat Offenders

16. How To Discover Your Divine Destiny and Total Breakthroughs

17. Church Without God: Exploit the truth and purge yourself in the faith

18. How To Discover Your Life Purpose, Cast Unique Vision And Goals: 12 Proven Techniques

19. 21 Keys to Miracles in Helpless Situations: How to pray when you can't pray

20. How To Make Heaven: Eliminating caricature, making the part straight

21. How To Break The Yoke Of Life: Finding your way to freedom, health, wealth and fulfillment

Thank you.

## MOSES OMOJOLA

Author of '**How To Discover Your Divine Destiny and Total Breakthroughs**' and many other great books.

**Visit:** www.jomakinspublishing.com

# ABOUT THE AUTHOR

I am the author of the popular book "How to discover your divine destiny and total breakthroughs" and over 20 other great books. I hold Bachelor and Masters Degree in Mining Engineering, also the Founding Pastor of Christ Intervention Ministries. I spent 16 years working as an Engineer in the Oil and Gas industry before I was divinely conscripted into my divine assignment. I am an Author, International Speaker, Counselor, Destiny and Life Purpose Mentor, Business and Wellness Coach. My Specialties are revealing Hidden Truths, Divine Assignment, Biblical Justice, Success and Leadership.

I run workshops and seminars helping people discover their destiny, life purpose, the unique business God created them to do, how to start and succeed. I also counsel individuals empathetically on issues relating to destiny, employment, health, relationships, and many more, tapping into the awesome power inherent in their destiny, and assist many to become writers and self – publish their books online in eBook, audiobook and paperback formats.

I hope you found the book useful. Please kindly go to the book page on Amazon and post a honest short review for me.

www.ingramcontent.com/pod-product-compliance
Lightning Source LLC
Chambersburg PA
CBHW072029190526
45166CB00015B/1419